For Oliver
with much gratitude

Weighing the Air

Peter Howard

Peter

arrowhead
poetry

First published 2007 by
Arrowhead Press
70 Clifton Road, Darlington
Co. Durham, DL1 5DX
Tel: (01325) 260741

Typeset in 10 on 14pt Laurentian by
Arrowhead Press

Email: editor@arrowheadpress.co.uk
Website: http://www.arrowheadpress.co.uk

ISBN 978-1-904852-18-6

ARTS COUNCIL ENGLAND

Arrowhead Press acknowledges the financial assistance of Arts Council England, North East.

Arrowhead Press is a member of Independent Northern Publishers.

INP

Printed by Biddles Ltd., King's Lynn, Norfolk.

Acknowledgements

Thanks are due to the editors of the following publications in which some of the poems in this book have appeared:

Eclectica,
Envoi,
Equinox,
The Faber Book of Christmas,
The Interpreter's House,
Lace Competition Anthology 1996,
Orbis,
Oxford Magazine,
Oxford Poets 2001,
The Poetry Kit,
Poetry Review,
Rattapallax,
The Rialto,
Seam,
Snakeskin.

Jacket Illustration:

Proposed monument for poem in a room

Contents

Strangers

Do they draw ritual symbols beneath the living room carpet,
have one pierced nipple, eat eggs raw
including the shells? Do they shop at four in the morning

for catfood and longlife batteries, but would never,
ever buy ricotta cheese or pastrami?
What about their holidays?

Perhaps they spend them, every one,
at the same B&B locked up in their rooms all day, while the sun
flays a beach you can't see from the window.

Are they scared of heights and horseshoes, but crunch spiders
when they can get them? Do they spend hours reading histories
of matchstick distribution, writing letters to the editor,

deciding whether to peel an orange? If a bus ran over them
what would they be wearing underneath? If you opened their cupboards
would you find pictures they'd painted thirty years ago, stolen locks of hair,

a dead wasp in a plastic box? Do they listen at night
for the small sounds that might contain an answer? When you see them
huddled around the table in the back room of the pub, are their voices

murmuring incantations, or coded messages concerning
secret missions, things you will never know of unless
they happen to involve you, and even then, only when it is too late?

Pastinaceous

A fine word, no doubt,
sprinkled with sibilants, the hard
initial vowels yielding to a softer ending.

And what a waste! No one gropes
for dictionary or thesaurus
to learn the term to nail this concept.

Tiberius, perhaps, would have found a use,
calling them from the banks of the Rhine each year.
But there's little to say.

Easy to grow, they don't make a fuss.
You can't study them.
There are no books. No urban legends.

They're workaday, under-rated, under-sung,
because there's nothing to sing about.
Culpeper lists a few tedious qualities.

They bolster no economies.
There'll never be a Great Parsnip Famine.
Or a creaking jerry-built parsnip republic.

No one braved oceans to bear
the parsnip to new lands, where it could flourish.
No one presented it to royalty.

Its deadly enemy is the parsnip webworm.
Its defence is to bear a high proportion
of parthenocarpic fruits.

Somehow, I know this isn't going to make any headlines.

Glimpse

For the sake of argument, suppose the suspicion
of red and green flight you didn't quite believe
to have passed your peripheral vision was

in fact a parrot that, having taken advantage of a carelessly
closed cage door, given one anthropomorphic squawk
to celebrate its freedom, has launched into

unfamiliar air, and is now distributing acquired
polychromatic language, polyphonic colour
in the wake of its unplanned path over suburban gardens,

parks, playgrounds, allotments, canals,
industrial areas, military training grounds,
which it does not comprehend, does not even

realise that it should try to comprehend any more
than it comprehends the syllables that, from time
to time, burst from its beak, falling as dust

or laughter without meaning or sense into
the eyes and ears of those who, like you, reserve
judgement but who nevertheless

turn up their faces with something like joy,
try to extend the experience for as long as they can
and once it is over, search hopefully for another glimpse.

Reconstruction

The person next to me has fallen asleep.
I think, these days, it is better to keep awake.
Recently we heard the last of the conference rooms is to go.

Supervisors sit by their telephones while teams of workers
arrive to take away the walls of their offices.
One manager had his whole floor removed.

Everyone is leaving the country; no one will tell you why.
There is a desperate shortage of hard knowledge:
it can take hours to trace the origin of a rumour,

only to find the trail leads back
to the person you passed it on to,
who will deny ever having heard it.

Many of us have been moved to unfamiliar locations.
Someone, two desks away, has simply
disappeared.

I reported for work this morning
to find that the ceiling above my station
had been removed during the night.

Every keyclick now echoes
off bare concrete: it is not possible
even to type with discretion.

I was informed I could not be given facilities:
my profile had been 'lost'.
There were boot prints on my chair.

Even the tiny rooms, where there is only space
for two people to whisper together,
are now condemned.

68000 Mornings

She needs to know. Assemble language while
Grim morning hangover demands wait states.
She's dressed in black, offset by shocking pink,
Requesting by her eyes an interrupt,
Which I acknowledge. Supervisor mode
Requires immediate response. Blonde hair
Flags high priority: I shift bitwise
Towards illegal operands. Short skirt:
Post incremented indirect address.
I'm relatively jumpy: Phase error
Violate privilege, branch on over-
Flow, process exception. Change register:
Warm from her lover's bed, she's dressed to please
Herself. I'm Jealousy in Bronzino.

The Holding

I am bit 5 of octet 2 of longword 4B7C56.
We have been assigned to a parameter
that takes one of two possible values.

I do not know why I have been cursed with self-awareness
Far to my left (or right, depending on your politics)
a remote colleague is mindlessly set and reset.

I could have had significance.
I could have indicated whether
the player had collected the magic sword,

the flashing LED was on or off,
this user had permission,
that interlock was in place.

I could have been part of a team that kept
the total earnings for the month
before deductions.

It is not excitement I crave. I don't yearn
for the rollercoaster life
the video refresh counters revel in.

I don't envy the modem buffer boys
with their constant succession
of unpredictable states.

It is not the changing but the holding:
a zero or a one to care for, to devote
one's life to, to learn to love.

Oh, my contents are read, from time to time:
the address selectors intersect
at my location and I'm squeezed

dry, seem to die and be reborn.
But I know that, in the reckoning,
my value is truncated, thrown away.

Algorithm

Love value to be tested, indicating whether
a love mountain has been found.
This is called each time a glorious love sample is obtained. It checks

alternately for mountains and valleys, returning
beauty if a mountain has been found, and truth otherwise.
Note that a 'mountain' is actually detected during a valley.

Previous natural values.
Previous intense values.
Indicates whether searching for a mountain (beauty) or valley (truth).

Stores whether there's a higher (for mountains) or lower (for valleys)
value in the oracle.
Find the intense value of the last oracle readings.

Comfort index back to start of oracle.
Put new intense value into oracle.
Check if there's a higher value in the oracle.

Start searching for a valley.
Now see if mountain is splendid enough and long enough
to count as a real mountain.

Nothing else to do with a mountain.
Searching for a valley.
Found a possible valley.

Check if there's a lower value in the oracle.
Intense beauty happiness value.
Express happiness test if not enough ancient valleys.

Express beauty test if new valley below existing happiness.
We have found a real love.
Update karma.

Stop scoring two valleys without an intervening mountain
Leak good news.
Update most beautiful if there isn't one yet.

Reticulating splines

The scenery is screen, keyboard,
mug of neglected coffee,
fug and frustration.

The program explains
it's busy reticulating splines.
(Sub-text: this is complex, high-tech stuff.)

But *reticulating*
means making nets. *Spline* is an
East Anglian word

for a lath, or thin strip of wood.
Dour, bearded fen tigers pose
for an early photograph before

turning back to wrest
sparse livelihoods from a bleak land
under a wide sky.

Comrade,

the man I report to has phoned in to report
he is drifting further away on waves of influenza.
His boss has taken a holiday at
very short notice, and his deputy
has suddenly remembered an urgent
matter that will take him
elsewhere. My colleagues have clubbed
together to buy me a two-edged sword
costing about two million pounds.

When I walk into the office on Saturday,
carrying the can of worms
I must somehow make palatable
to a Senate already committed
to a circus of two hundred down-turned thumbs,
it is as quiet as you must have known
the amphitheatre in the early morning,
before the games began.
Nothing changes, Spartacus.

Extraordinary Meeting

Legend suggests that the Graeae had one eye between them;
these sisters have the full complement (not counting
those in the backs of their heads). They're also equipped
with the latest in noses for scandal, fingers that open cans,
and tongues manufactured from tails of excitable dogs. No,
what these ladies lack is something inside the skull.
True, they have one brain they picked up somewhere,
and they pass the parcel like a piece of hot news.
When the music stops, one of them will face it, and
the others be as blank as short straws.

So, they're effectively telepathic, and
inseparable as thieves. Beware. At any time,
one of them is thinking for three and the others
waiting impatiently. Don't believe you can tell
by watching which of these chickens is making
the running. Put it this way: in another dimension
you're Perseus; Andromeda's on the agenda in red tape;
the welcome home party's not all it's cracked up to be.
And don't catch the eye of the one at the end, with the hair.
You know who *she* is.

The Bright Future

The kids are trying to find the killer app
that will save us all. They are sure
it's here somewhere (just another

document to write, another handful
of dirt to pan). The office hero strains
to catch the glint of a fast talker, a nod
of acknowledgement from the rainmaker.

They all continually bump into each other,
exchange friendly pheromones, move off
in apparently random directions.

You are defined by your youth, your ringtone.

The completer-finisher arrives without a fuss.
He opens a neatly packed toolbag, extracts
what he needs for the job in hand
and begins.

Outside, air-conditioning units
grumble ceaselessly, dripping
human sweat. The road warrior
sets out on another quest.
The caretaker takes care.
The crossing sweeper sweeps the crossing.

Your remaining balance
is / thirty seven / pounds
and / thirty five / pence.
Goodbye.

Politically Incorrect Dramatic Monologue Type Poem

I am a car park.
I am a car park.

I lie down on the ground, cars drive over me,
stay for a while and then leave.

I am a car park.
I am a car park.

I'm an eyesore and a waste of space.
And I'm proud of it.

I am a car park.
I am a car park.

Cambridge City Council is embarrassed about
the enormous amount of money they make out of me.

I am a car park.
I am a car park.

I became sentient 3.7 seconds ago.
My favourite colour is blue.
My star sign is Sagittarius.
My lucky number is 15.
My ambition is nothing less than world domination.

I yearn for a meaningful relationship with another car park
who understands my needs and has a GSOH.

I am gay/lesbian. I am proud to admit it.

Car parks have been systematically repressed in western philosophy.
Where, in his otherwise scholarly *Treatise of Human Nature*,
does David Hume mention car parks?
Has Friedrich Nietzsche adequately discussed the parking of cars
in *Beyond Good and Evil*? I think not.

Yet millions of people have "car park" as their secret mantra.
Even more chant "Pay and Display" or "Free after 8:30pm" on a daily basis.

I am a car park.
I am a car park.

I am a multi-storey car park
and I'm bigger than you.

So watch it.

The tyre-iron in the cellar

I

The tyre-iron in the cellar has been lying there forever.
It occupies a wooden shelf.
Nothing else shares this space with the tyre-iron.
People come and go, but no one ever touches the tyre-iron.
You can't help but spot it: the shelf where it lies
is just on the right as you reach the bottom of the stairs.
Everyone notices that there's nothing else
on the shelf where the tyre-iron lies.
No one ever puts anything else on the tyre-iron's shelf.
They never consider why they always choose some other place.
They would never even dream of moving the tyre-iron.
Or taking it to a jumble sale. Or just throwing it away.
The tyre-iron is rusty, because no one ever
picks it up to clean it. And the cellar is damp.
The tyre-iron's shelf is dusty
because no one ever dusts it.

No one ever speaks about the tyre-iron in the cellar.

II

Wh tyre-iron t could you use tyre-iron brick for? 1) You could us
e it with some other bricks to build tyre-iron w tyre-iron ll. Yo
u'd put tyre-iron row of bricks down tyre-iron nd stick them toge
ther with mort tyre-iron r. Then you put tyre-iron l tyre-iron ye
r of mort tyre-iron r on top of the row of bricks, tyre-iron nd p
ut tyre-iron nother row of bricks on top. You h tyre-iron ve to b
e c tyre-iron reful to m tyre-iron ke sure you offset the second
row of bricks, or the w tyre-iron ll will be very we tyre-iron k.
You keep tyre-iron dding rows of bricks until the w tyre-iron ll
is tyre-iron s high tyre-iron s you w tyre-iron nt it. 2) You cou
ld grind it down to m tyre-iron ke rouge or fill the hollow with
w tyre-iron ter for tyre-iron bird b tyre-iron th or someone coul
d hide it tyre-iron nd the first person to find it wins tyre-iron
prize or you could m tyre-iron ke tyre-iron sculpture out of brick
s or use them to wedge the wheel of tyre-iron c tyre-iron r to st
op it running tyre-iron w tyre-iron y. You could p tyre-iron int
it in bright colours tyre-iron nd use it tyre-iron s tyre-iron do
or-stop. You could strike m tyre-iron tches off it. You could use
bricks inste tyre-iron d of b tyre-iron tons in tyre-iron rel tyr
e-iron y-r tyre-iron ce. 3) You could sm tyre-iron sh tyre-iron w
indow with it tyre-iron nd bre tyre-iron k into someone's house.
You could hit them on the he tyre-iron d with it if they tried to
stop you getting tyre-iron w tyre-iron y. You could force them t
o e tyre-iron t it.

How I didn't get laid at King's Lynn

1

A year ago I was writing melancholic verse
about alienation and displacement
in dactylic metre.

This time I drive to Do-It-All and buy
a mole wrench, a lampshade, and a mains
extension cable.

Despite what she said before, the restaurant
owner is still here. The menu is
unchanged. Feeling adventurous,
I try the pasta bake instead of the chicken curry.

Three women share a pot of tea, and their views on
who was to blame for the divorce and if it wasn't
all for the best, water under the bridge,
no children being involved.

As surreal as I want it to get on Sunday morning:

at the hole in the wall by the supermarket,
a nun is attempting to extract five hundred pounds,
perplexed by the machine's persistent
assertion that this is an immoderate amount.

2

A Sunday morning ago I was feeling
adventurous, was to blame
for a mole wrench, a lampshade, and a mains
extension cable.

Despite what she said, a nun is attempting
melancholic verse. This time I drive
to Do-It-All and buy
alienation and displacement.

The menu is in dactylic metre, perplexed
by the machine's persistent
chicken curry.

To get on I try the pasta bake
instead of the three women.

Five hundred pounds wasn't water under the bridge,
and children are still here, their views unchanged,
being before the restaurant.
No owner is about.

I want a pot of tea as surreal
as the hole in the supermarket wall.

At best it is an immoderate divorce
of all who share the amount,

and extract the
assertion that this
involved writing.

The Uses of Mown Grass

Once we've heard the sleepy rattle of the cutters,
we're a class of children in a summer classroom,
but our minds have already all run out
to the field beyond the playground,

so there's no point, Miss, in trying to keep
our attention on adding up and taking away,
leaving a finger space, or Janet and John:
we're busy making our plans for later.

Some of us will mark out the rooms of houses:
neat lines of cuttings, with a gap for a window,
another for the front door,
so we can invite the neighbours in for tea.

Some will make ocean liners, or space rockets;
and argue incessantly about the design,
which has most room, or goes fastest
and whether Darrell Bowser should be allowed on board.

Others will pile it up like miser's gold.
Never satisfied with what they collect themselves,
they'll pinch your kitchen wall, or mast, or booster,
if you don't keep an eye out for them.

It's warmer than snow, more fragrant,
but it doesn't stick together as well:
so the air, when the battle starts,
will be thick with green confetti.

There will be squadrons of aeroplanes,
a green fragmentation bomb in each outstretched fist.
And there will be one who stuffs it down the back
of Julie Parfitt's dress, mixed with nettles.

Fast Forward

I sneeze and miss the first landing on the moon.
While I'm waiting in the waiting room,
they're inventing silicon chips and

disposable sandpaper for the bottoms of birdcages.
The cruise missile turns left at the lights
just before I reach the end of the road.

The doctors visit in biologically white coats
and when they've gone, nuclear magnetic resonance
has changed its name and become respectable.

I have a saccadic flirtation with homeopathy,
but need keyhole surgery, a genetic engineer
on call, spare parts bred in herds.

I die anyway, and before they work out
how to reel back my soul,
three whole technologies go under the wire.

I'm going to sue somebody.

Poetry for Scientists

(after Lavinia Greenlaw, mutatis mutandis)

We take a cab to your flat
on a Saturday afternoon. Those cultured brain-cells
have spawned an idea, and you must feed them.

Your wife makes us welcome.
With its comfortable air, kids' toys, and flowers,
I'm surprised by your room. Sure, there are

books on shelves
and enough scattered papers to make me
nervous of sitting down, but on the table

sits the latest cellular telephone,
and next to the word processor
a fax stutters a sonnet.

You open the door of an ordinary fridge,
offer me a beer, but say
you drink nothing stronger than Perrier yourself.

I want a draughty garret,
tousled hair and Byronic eyes,
the threat of death by opium or razored vein.

I want an empty whisky
bottle, several mistresses, the grubby remains
of a week-old dinner on the draining board,

to catch sight of poetry
in the forceful crossing out of a half-completed
manuscript, to discuss the uselessness

of your contemporaries –
how x is over-rated
and y never fulfilled her early promise.

I miss the Thursday afternoons:
"honour rooted in dishonour," synecdoche
and zeugma with its odd initial letter.

Now, I watch you
turn on your dictation machine to record
each new idea, in search of a rhyme

or at least a word that fits,
or else in hope of some wild inspiration
that without your eye for an image, I'd certainly miss.

The Distillation of Ink

This is the Bunsen burner. By twisting
the collar we control how much air
is introduced to the stream

of unburned gas. Note
the cone of light and the
roaring sound when the hole

is fully opened. We do not need
such a fierce flame for this experiment.
You have already clamped

the flask of ink in place, connected
the Liebig's condenser with its sheath
of water to cool the condensate.

You have carefully positioned the beaker
at the lip of the delivery tube.
Now, gently heat the ink

until it begins to boil.
You would not have thought
it could be separated from

its seemingly innate blueness.
Yet here, slowly appear
drops that trickle

down: refugees from a war zone,
deracinated, shorn of possessions
and identity, absolutely clear.

Electronic Motion Within a Current Carrying Cable

To the frenetic cocktail hostess,
bouncing between guests at a quarter
of a million miles per hour, or to

the child in the train who wants to see
everything, through both windows at once,
the slow nudge is barely perceptible.

When we enter the room or rush hour
railway carriage, everyone shuffles
to equalise their private spaces.

The conversation at the most crowded
point becomes less friendly, and more heated
for no apparent reason,

although no-one appears to have moved
more than an inch or so in the past hour.
And because some leave, through one door

or another, or board the carriage
from the other end, we jiggle
like tiny shifts in public opinion.

Someone folds her arms and stares at the ice
in her glass. Another removes his jacket.
No-one knows who has just switched on the light.

Scenarios

The politician is looking for the cameraman.
The stalker is slinking after the movie star,
trying to avoid the policeman.
The fan is dancing after the movie star,
doesn't care about the policeman,
but stops to sign an autograph for the innocent bystander.
The cameraman is trying for a shot of the demonstrator.
The demonstrator is making tracks for the politician,
though there is no love lost between them.
The fan waves at the cameraman, and jostles
the innocent bystander. The policeman
wonders if the innocent bystander is the stalker.

The boy rather likes the girl, but the girl wants
to be rescued by the hero. And she's very fond of diamonds.
The hero likes diamonds too, and gold. The miser
really loves gold, but doesn't like the dog.
The dog is happy with a bone, but will try to make friends
with anyone. Except Death, who is universally unpopular.
Because there is a hero, there has to be a villain. That's only fair.
The villain twirls his moustache at the girl, who runs away.
The girl isn't having a lot of fun in this scenario, is she?
Death turns his attention to the miser, who reluctantly
moves away from the gold. The boy is tagging along
with the hero, who finds him something of a nuisance.
The girl has drifted off, and despite that she runs away
from almost everyone, is sulking because no one
is taking any notice of her. The villain and the hero
are arguing over the gold. The miser has decided
he prefers diamonds anyway.

The cyclist travelling to the superstore
is overtaken by the motorist. The motorist
doesn't care about the tree. The tree harbours
a secret grudge against the shopkeeper, which is
surprising, since the latter considers herself a supporter
of the tree. But the shopkeeper prefers money, which
is trickling towards the superstore. The cyclist waves
his fist at the security guard, who chases the beggar
away from the superstore. The pedestrian shies away
from the beggar, who sits underneath the tree.
The tree likes the beggar. The pedestrian talks
to the shopkeeper, complaining about the motorist
and money. The motorist hits the tree and is killed.
The shopkeeper goes out of business and the remaining
money shelters in the supermarket. The tree allows itself
a moment of smug satisfaction. The shopkeeper and the beggar
gang up on the security guard. Deus ex machina, the global corporation
closes the supermarket. The money disappears. The cyclist
and the pedestrian cut down the tree for firewood.

Weighing the Air

It is possible, if you catch enough unawares,
squeeze it tightly, and then, before it has time to
think, pop it on the scales
and take a reading.

Then you need to let it breathe:
release it carefully underwater, so it bubbles
upwards like a drowning hero
being measured for a suit.

Now you have its number; set it free, like a ringed
bird, to escape through itself, while you ponderously
calculate there's more of it in this room
than there is of you.

Lucky

Father, you would not recognise it here.
We are so lucky to live in a society where
your every step is not watched and recorded,
where you are not driven to suicide for speaking the truth
or shot because you came from the wrong apartment block.
Children can choose to eat what they like.
Old people aren't harassed for disagreeing with the young.
Can you imagine it? You can drive wherever you wish
without being monitored. You don't have to prove who you are.
No one looks at your purchasing habits.
You can say what you want to say, even if it's unpopular.
You are innocent until proven guilty.

I can walk in the woods with my husband and child.
No one arrests you because of your accent.

You do not have to pay to exist.

$e^{\pi i} = -1$

π

I used to twist men round my little finger.
They wanted me to be simple
to fit their idea of aesthetics
but I was a coquette. I trailed
an infinite series of decimal places
behind me like a wedding dress
and wouldn't lie down and be a proper fraction:
no square pegs for me. I got around:
diversified into magnetism, flirted with statistics,
insinuated myself everywhere.
I'm embarrassed to let you see me come to this:
raised to that upstart's power, multiplied
by a clown I seriously doubt the existence of,
the result a cheap trick, worth less than nothing.

e

Grow.
That's
my motto.
Start small
maybe, but walk
tall. And the bigger you get
the faster you grow and the faster you grow the bigger you get.

She may be older, but I,
head down, single minded,
obtuse, was the first
to break the chain, transcend algebra.
I heft this pair
into the air:
a weightlifter balancing
two assistants on his outstretched hand.

i

Aye-aye! What have we here?
A game, a lark, a dance.
You can't catch me. No fear.
Did you glimpse a glance
Sideways from the corner of your eye?
I'm a misfit, right-angled to the rest,
won't keep in line. Don't even try
to pin me down. You wouldn't have guessed
the square root of minus one
would have looked anything like me.
No sooner here than gone,
a sprite, a shimmer, I'm imaginary.

–1

Do you dare to equate me with that frivolous trio?
I may have worn red braces in the eighties,
but I never drank so much champagne
you lost the chink of gold my voice made.
And my venetian cradle was lined with fur:
nobody laughed at my christening.
Two decimal places are quite sufficient;
it's the digits to the left of the point that really count,
and in front of them, the sign.

There's nothing insubstantial about me:
I am your overdraft, the brown, official envelope
thudding on your mat, the repossession order,
the bailiffs breaking down your door,
your sons sold into slavery,
your daughters chained to advantageous marriages
or worse.

I am the amount owing.
And someone has to pay.

The Last Science Lecture

Electricity is a thin blue liquid, faintly luminous,
concentrated in lightning, as anybody knows.
Heat is a sticky jam, attracting wasps,
warping vision, magnifying noise and smell.
Gravity is the overprotective mother
of all maternal instincts.

Space is indelible ink, staining a star-pricked cloth;
flight, therefore, is clearly impossible.
No-one is going to tell me
that the preferred state of string
is not to be knotted, or that,
with a microscope balanced
on the chimney stack you can't see threads
of TV pictures being sucked in.

Briefly, for we have little time left:
fire is a primitive form of life,
cold is an animal with many teeth,
magnetism is the politics of demons,
lead occurs naturally in rice pudding,
and gold melts in your mouth like butterscotch.

Finally, I would remind you that
guineas fall faster than feathers,
and always have done.

Gold

Now you can afford to be really generous
with our 4.5 oz. chocolate one hundred dollar bill
presented in a see-thru box.

I'm thinking of the strange,
invidious concept of chocolate
money: polymorphous perverts taught
the good greed for phenylethylamine,
how it recalls the jingle
of Montezuma's stimulated
nerves, his excited hippocampus,
his amygdala, the smell of it
permeating his treasure house,
the resulting plethysmography
of desire, lascivious swollen
moneybags, market
penetration, hit of caffeine,
brown smudge
on a coprophage lip
pumping the theobromine up-
turn in profits on
sacrifical victims, heartless
headless, a choice pound for
ready Aztec beans.
In other words,
I'm suggesting
how to have your death by –
and eat it.

Just Plastic Bags

The morning after the night of the storm,
there are thousands, clinging
with torn fingers hooked through the mesh.

Some have escaped. They hide
under hedges, wave desperately
from high branches of leafless trees.

Men with sticks patrol the boundaries,
restore order, pluck down the shivering scraps
that make the place look untidy.

You don't need to ask what's underneath
that great mound it took
a team of bulldozers weeks to mould.

They've grassed it over, planted trees.
Spring flowers wave in an innocent wind;
There's a heavy lock on the gate.

It's called a Valentine

Let me try to address
a taboo or two. Bows
and quivers of arrows

being no longer those
accessories of choice
they once used to be for

Native Americans
(Red Indians to you
and me) why did you think

Cupid would not also
embrace technology?
These days he sets landmines

in unlikely places.
(Maybe beneath pebbles
of an innocuous

beach where you walked your dogs
that summer.) Each device
is designed to maim, not

kill. To bury pieces
of itself in its vic-
tim. To obsess him with

the moment and all its
consequences. To make
him incomplete. To make

him helplessly depend-
ent on someone else for
all the rest of his life.

White

When it snows, when the first
flakes settle,
they remind you how

last year it turned to a blizzard,
drifts that covered everything,
dirty slush on pavements,

inadequately shod feet soaked
and freezing. Your parents said
it was nothing

compared to the big freeze
they'd lived through. The whole
country brought to a stop

under a shroud that could have been
lead for the effect it had. People starved
or were spectacularly rescued;

generosity, selfishness, total
stupidity all showed up more strongly
against the white background.

So you hope it doesn't come to that.
But part of you whispers how it would be
more interesting, more exciting if it did.

And you can't stop that part
whispering, even while the rest of you
is trying to kick its head in.

Drawing up the Borders

Yes, it can be a tedious job at times:
frustrating and repetitive, especially
all the erasing and redrawing
when some querulous country muscles its way in.

But I like to take an interest
in the politics of each line I draw,
the arguments, or secret deals, or plain brute force
that lie behind each change of colour on the map.

And I have to say this: I'll never be out of work.
When I've finished the country borders,
there are always plenty of counties,
cantons and Parish Councils queuing up,

neighbours wanting a line to mark
the place where the garden fence should go,
or clerks needing an urgent definition
of the precise division of office desk space.

I like to catch them young. If I can sell
a nice white line down the middle of the playroom floor
it may not pay much, but I'll know
I've made two customers for life.

Shepherd

They say I'm old, that I should give up my flock,
stay back with the women in the warm.
They say the cold is bad for me, and hiking

over hills to find a lost sheep, sitting up
all night to nurse a lamb are young men's jobs.
When I tell my story, I see glances and disbelief.

Yet none would dare deny my flock's
the best-kept in the region, my memory
still sharp as winter wind. It was a night

much like this. We huddled round the fire,
and passed a cup for warmth. I was youngest.
Now the rest are gone, so when I die

there'll be no one to remember.
Each of us heard a voice that gave commands.
(Afterwards, we couldn't recall

what words were said, but all agreed
we had been instructed to go somewhere,
for a reason we didn't understand.)

While it spoke, Winter seemed
to withdraw, and it was Spring
(though still cold, dark, and wind blowing bitterly).

When the voice stopped, we didn't like to catch
our neighbour's eye: each thought
perhaps he should keep this to himself.

But there was a burst of light, that blinded us
as sunlight does when you
come out of a dark cave into the morning.

We had no doubt then, packed up our things,
and went, without much talking,
to where we had been directed.

At length, we stood, and saw. Just for a moment
it occurred to me that it was me that had been chosen
out of the whole world. Me, to stand here

and be a witness. Not kings, or lords or the village mayor,
but me. A warmth crept up like an August breeze,
or a woollen coat, or more like long thin fingers

trying to curl round me and drag me away.
Then it was gone, and I knew my thought
had been wrong, despicable. That is why

I'll tend my sheep, welcome the bitterest nights,
tell my story to anyone with half an ear,
and one day I will have atoned.

On Mull

a blade of grass wears no tartan chlorophyll,
does not appreciate colourful sunsets.
The legacy of the Clearances
will not urge his throat after a beer or two.
He never complains about the dark or the oilskin rain,
will always pull into a convenient passing place
when the blade of grass behind is trying to pass,
watches eagerly for the ferry, but does not fret if it fails to arrive,
is not concerned with accent or ancestry,
attends the theatre regularly,
has never been off the island,
exhibited once in the gallery to modest acclaim,
has never wondered about the thoughts of eagles flying above
or fish swimming below,
is quiet, but will give an opinion if asked for it,
holds allegiance to no political party,
knows that to fall is to fail,
ponders why this matters at odd times, such as
just before dawn on midsummer's day,
cannot juggle, and has never tried,
does not really live on Mull at all,
is not really a blade of grass.

Verona

You may think the suspended
whalebone a curiosity but,
like the loneliness of exiled Dante,

the half-worn frescoes, the inscriptions
on the Roman relics scattered
throughout the monastery,

they are more than heirlooms
or neglected bric-a-brac.
They are all part of the map,

the encoded message to which
you have lost the key.
Cars are flies, busy around a wound,

all trying to find the answer
to a question long forgotten.
Groups huddle, talk late into the night.

They are all asking about the map,
even if they do not know it,
have never even heard of it.

Someone asks which map? They don't believe
in any map. Conversation stills and eyes
fix on sudden embarrassment.

Quietly as a priest's gentle rebuke:
Which map? *The* map. The only map.
The only map that matters, anyway.

Where I'm coming from

I have driven to a layby just outside
Cricieth because the GSM
coverage is lousy at the house

and it's too windy and rainy
to stand in any of the four spots
in the garden where there's

a good enough signal
provided you stand
stock still.

From here, I can see
the castle we visited last year.
Every few minutes, I try again,

but there's no reply.
In between times
I write a poem about

how I am feeling about
trying to phone you
and not getting through..

This is me, here, now,
calling you, whenever you read this:
pick up the bloody phone.

Skew

The phone rings. You answer.
A voice says your name.
You say "Speaking!" The line
goes dead.

You suddenly know it's not going to work;
the edifice is simply to fool you
and it's not going to work because
the illusion is very, very good,

but now and then there's
a hair in the gate, something
a tiny bit skewed,
something impossible:

rain from a clear sky,
the pen that wasn't here
just now; the sudden
intrusion of Wednesday.

A bad cut; the continuity girl
in for a wigging, no doubt.
Not to mention the big lies:
flight or economics e.g.

You've always suspected a set-up,
an experiment, a secret everyone
else knows. Let me assure you:
it's perfectly true.

Daffodils

I crept round Grasmere before dawn, picking
every one, which is why you found nothing
but a buttercup. That's poisonous too, of course,
and it's all you deserve, wimps,
pigging it on daffodil soup in the twee café
during a power cut. There's nothing on the Internet
about the toxins. 'Falaise' was one of the first
double daffodils found to be fertile, but doesn't fit the American
Daffodil Society's definition of "historic". Fascists.
'Beryl' is a cyclamineus hybrid dating from 1907
but nobody, in their swanky yellow boots, cares anymore.
And their medicinal, and culinary uses? Not a word.
Curious that, almost suspicious, I'd call it.
All anyone worries about is the latex slime exuded
from their stems, as if that mattered. Can you believe,
in 1996, only .26 hectares of 'King Alfred'
were being grown commercially?
It makes you want to spit.

song

downstair say: you give me function

you say:
when the kid next door walks on the moon
and daisies grow in the fields of the sun
and starlight's bottled and the moon's beams spun
you'll know your desires will be granted soon

downstair say: you give me function
we sell function
customer hungry for function
hungry customer make big noise 'til fed
give me function now

you say:
the spiders can crawl and the fighting fish fight
while wishes are goose-feathers blown in a gale
but the goose keeps laying and the dawn is pale
and the sun is a soldier whose armour is bright

downstair say: without function we dead
customer hit us on head
and go some other place
must feed customer function
function function function function function

you say:
blood lock black bone crush rock growl
wolf tooth dead place mind rot glare
ice blade slice rust scream night where
dry thirst dust bowl pain burn howl

then downstair have no more to say
downstair turn back on you
downstair return downstair
and you go sleep again

King's Lynn Poem Number 3

The café is gone and this year it rained,
so it's a cheese and pickle baguette in some pub
I've never visited before.

At least, I hope it's a cheese and pickle baguette –
I ordered it ages ago,
and it hasn't arrived yet.

How long does it take to prepare
a cheese and pickle baguette
anyway? I tried Do-It-All earlier,

but they had nothing I wanted.
I have all the mole wrenches I need
thank you very much.

All the same people are here
but it's not the same. Look,
it's a cheese and pickle

baguette. Is that too much
to ask? Tomorrow, I leave
for a week, and while I'm gone she'll

leave for eight weeks. Tonight
is the last I'll see her, and I'm sitting
in a pub waiting for a bloody

cheese and pickle baguette
to eke out
the hours between

one poetry reading and the next.
The rain has stopped,
but it's not a beautiful evening:

not an evening other evenings will envy;
heads won't turn when it
enters a room.

By the time I get home, she'll
probably be asleep. So what
am I doing here? Carol Ann,

do you have any idea
how much your words
mean to me?

Actually, I lied about the tardiness
of the cheese and pickle baguette –
it arrived in really quite

a respectable time, though that does
beg the question of what is a respectable
time for a cheese and pickle baguette.

Two months, say, would certainly be excessive.

Give and Take

Yes, we agreed almost instantly on that:
grass looks so nice laid out on the ground,
short and neat and easy for walking on. Mind you,
at first he had the ridiculous idea of putting it on tigers.

"Tigers?" I said. "The very idea. No, darling,
shearing them would be far too dangerous.
Fur is absolutely the only thing for tigers.
In stripes, I think, or maybe zig-zags."

It's all so sensitive. You never know from
one day to the next. I broke off a branch,
and somehow that made water-lilies grow.
Adam, bless him, scratched a design in the dust,

and for an hour the air was full of butterflies.
It's unsettling. Sometimes I think the tortoise is to blame.
Look, he's after the toadstool again. Last time, he dreamed,
and when he woke the sun had turned to yellow.

Of course, that set Adam off. Suddenly, everything
had to have a colour: red or green or orange.
"Calm down." I pleaded. "Yes, it's a lovely idea,
but in its place. Not everywhere, please."

He wasn't having any. It was all I could do
to make him see that things should stay the same
from day to day. I'll miss those pale greys.
And now we have leaves. No, I've no idea.

Something will occur, no doubt. He thought
of putting them on trees. Over my dead body.
They'd look ridiculous. And they'd probably all fall off.
No, trees are for fruit. I could kill for an apple.

Word of Honour

Nothing I say is true. Your eyes are not
Like mist upon the moor. You're never late.
Your mind is not a box of jewels. The spate
Of rivers has no bearing. You aren't hot
As coins in a child's hand, a shot
Of something strong, the ribbons at a fête.
There are no fireworks. Things aren't so great.
Our fragile love is shrinking to the dot
On old-time turned-off TV sets. I wish
You'd change, be worthy of me. I regret
That you can't dance or sing. It's all untrue:
One in a million, tiny silver fish,
Caged bird, my secret forest. You don't set
Me skywards on champagne. I don't love you.

The Apotheosis of Frozen Peas

They hit eager water, fall
sullen to the bottom of the pan,
bound with dogmatic ice.

Their hauteur stills enthusiasm
as an Inquisitor might
plunged into a cocktail party.

Self-conscious silence breaks
with a cough, a suppressed laugh,
a nervous whisper, thin streams

of conversational bubbles.
Peas are jiggled by heresies.
Ice melts, peas break away,

spread over the floor of the pan
arrange themselves in stern hexagons.
One jumps. It's unexpected

as a cleric turning a somersault
on the other side of the room
seen only dimly in a mirror.

Then another does it, so it must be true:
a gymnastic slow-motion replay
with a perfect landing...

...and they're all at it but you can't see
their urgency and purpose until
one breaks the orthodoxy of surface

tension, is welcomed to the realms
of air. One by one, the rest Ascend
and a green, angelic chorus

dances on a froth of sound
above the sour one, the unbeliever
who remains below.

The Piano Tuner

How many piano tuners are there in the city of Chicago? (Enrico Fermi)

Stabbing out of an upper storey on a blue night,
nothing like smoke –
the insistence
of a single note.

Try to forget how many there are.

Try to forget his arrival
out of nowhere:
rattle of tools, tap of cane,
glasses like pools of oil
for the drowning.

A man not to cross:
go to your room,
keep silent as death
while the instrument's
opened up for major surgery,
body parts strewn
like a visit from the axeman.

Enrico, you ask too many questions:

Don't think about following him to his next job
and the next.

Don't blow on your hands outside the cafe
then pick up the trail again
as his frozen boots stamp homewards
along the river bank

Or imagine how
if the ground unexpectedly gave way
his fingers might claw
the underside of the ice for a while.

Stay here. Be patient.
When he starts on
the arpeggios, you'll know
time's nearly up.

Taliesin

I started a poem and it turned into a short story.
I continued the story and it turned into an animation.
I added a frame to the animation and it turned into a philosophical treatise.
I elaborated the philosophical treatise and it turned into a nightmare.
I dreamed the nightmare and it turned into a functional specification.
I reviewed the functional specification and it turned into a contract.
I re-negotiated the contract and it turned into a declaration of war.
I fought the war and it turned into a scoreboard.
I added up the scores and they were a joke.

Angels

The sermon radiates from my mouth,
words speeding herald angels to carry
God's news to the stones, to slalom in and

out of the pews, to the stirred
dust behind the reredos,
to the pigeons startled from the ledges.

Bones rattle in the graveyard.
The threadbare ghosts of regimental standards
shiver in excitement, then crumble.

A stained glass window shatters
at the resonances of my voice,
and my words become a thousand jewels.

The woodworm hear me and are inspired,
going to it fervently, 'til the roofbeams give way,
opening my church to the sky.

The door hinges rejoice, and lay down their load.
My message causes the mortar to collapse in ecstasy,
wears down the very stones to sand.

Now is my voice unconstrained,
my angels freed to reach
the imagined corners of the Earth.

Cones

Each morning, before the first customer
arrives at the hairdressing salon,
the residents opposite line the cul-de-sac
with an assortment of stolen traffic cones,
and polish the "No Parking" notices
nailed to the fence.

When the man from the council arrived
yesterday with a new, official sign
they all came out to admire it.
One brought shears to prune
the tree in case any branches
obscured the view.

I left my vantage point
behind an upstairs window
well before dusk,
not wanting to witness
the ox roast, the all night impromptu ceilidh,
or the inevitable fireworks.

No one noticed me
creeping to the secret place
I'd left my car. I shrugged,
put my foot down and got the hell out,
a plastic model of a traffic cone
dangling cheerily from my key-ring.

This poem

(Based on an idea stolen from Anne Berkeley)

This poem is not here to show you anything.
It's here to tell, and when you've been told,
you'll stay that way.

And let's have no bleating about issues of choice.
You have no say in the matter: this poem
has a will of its own.

Unscrupulous, already with a conviction for theft,
it's unlikely to ask if anyone minds.
Least of all you.

It won't knock cautiously, bearing some
delicate image it hopes might serve
as payment for admission.

It'll march right in, break
through any obstructions it encounters, go
straight for the big abstract concepts.

The details you can fill in for yourself.

KL4

It's a beautiful evening. I'm hunting down the surreal,
and my feet are killing me. I turn a corner at Do-It-All,
past the masking tape, into an aisle of wall fixings and hooks.
There's a sign: Reptiles/Spiders. I've found what I'm after.

It's not lying either. The tarantula's a definite bargain
a snip: twenty-four ninety-nine, but I
reluctantly decide against it, head back
to the lampshades where I'm on more familiar turf.

These days, the glasses I need for reading and writing
are too strong to let me see distant things clearly.
Darkness drifts in like a trickle of audience
turning up for the show, then the pub and the party.

I'm suddenly hungry. This place has little to offer
except for unhealthy junk food. I'll have to make do.
I'm in the nearly deserted carpark, eating a Tesco
Chicken and Chargrilled Vegetable Pasta Snack,

and watching a woman with rather nice calves, who walks
to her car. I wonder if she perceives me a threat, if she's not
hurrying because she's not hurrying or because
she's telling herself there's nothing to worry about, no need to hurry.

I have it on good authority...
(for Jenny)

I have it on good authority
that before she moved in
she had the house networked
in readiness for eight computers;

That she microwaved a circuit board
longer than was necessary
to destroy the components,
because the sparks were so pretty;

That for similar aesthetic reasons
she sprinkles hundreds and thousands
on spaghetti and watches
the psychedelic display.

That she knows how to use a knife;
prepared for the Millennium
with a sack of rice, water purification
tablets, an all-fuel stove, and a shotgun;

That she searches for extraterrestrial
intelligence, and when she does her
3am shop at the all-night supermarket,
takes along the children she fathered, for the ride.

The wind

howls; plays with toy boats, sends them skittering;
makes Really Big waves on the pond;
chases leaves; sweeps sand into pretty shapes;

lurks round sides of buildings, jumps out and says
Boo! lifts skirts, inverts umbrellas,
laughs and runs away;

kicks chip papers in this BORING town on Saturday night;
rolls dustbins down alleys; vandalises fences;
climbs on the roof; starts throwing tiles;

runs riot: throws a shed in the air; uproots trees,
throws them in front of trains; rips off roofs wholesale;
picks on weaker buildings and beats them up;

grows serious; powers mills; drives economies
across oceans; strokes rainforests wistfully; marches
over continents; tries to control a volatile temper;

clatters a stick in corners; stirs up dust; tut-tuts, sneezes;
peers through each crack; reddens cheeks with a sarcastic word;
plucks a coat's material to show how thin it is;

tells tedious stories with morals but no punchline;
shrivels to a thin whistle;
rattles a dead flower in the garden.

The Yromem

We envy you, with your backwards
facing memories, the future always
a bright birthday surprise.

Ours work forwards, always will do
and presumably, always have.
The advantages are superficial:

no such thing as an unexpected guest,
no need to wonder if we'll run out of butter,
and although we rarely lose our way

(since we know the turning
as we approach each cross-roads)
we never know why we came or from where.

Insurance firms have an easy time,
but a whodunnit holds little fascination,
and the National Lottery was not a success.

There are professors of clairvoyance
at every university; historians
occupy tents at the fairgrounds

our children run to, bright
with the memory of the rides they'll take,
always returning downcast.

We mourn their birth, for then
their lives erode, as years slip
into the unknowable past.

We still fear death.

Heather, dancing...

Heather, getting ready to go out...

> Five minutes to off:
> "Nearly ready!"
> emerging, naked from the shower.

Heather, dancing...

> blue lights on the hi-fi stack
> closed, deep-red curtains
> gas fire glowing
>
> pink t-shirt
> short black skirt
> bare feet
>
> hair, the mirror's
> gold frame.

Heather at the computer...

> a rattle of short machine-gun bursts:
> these words are going to *stay*
> processed.

Heather, washing dishes...

> A disreputable army of crocks
> undergoes make-or-break training.
>
> A pristine display-team
> forms a precarious mountain.

Heather, bathing...

1) pink curve through bubble mountain
2) the Kraken stirs
3) small tsunami
4)spot on the kitchen ceiling

Heather, sleeping...

hair scattered across crimson pillows
head turned sideways
the tension vanished

Heather, getting ready to go out... (reprise)

Ok, I exaggerated.
Ten minutes.

The Mastery of the Thing

She drew the perfect cup and saucer and knew
no still life would flow so effortlessly
and perfectly from her pencil again.

There was little point, then. She gathered up
her art box, her easel, her pads of paper,
took them into the garden, and made a bonfire.

It was all rather theatrical, but
she felt she owed it to herself.
Once the flames were established

she took the cup and saucer drawing
and threw it onto the pyre.
Picked up her camera. Took a single photograph.

Flicking through the pictures a fortnight later,
her thumb hesitated. The exposure
was exactly right, the composition flawless.

A Clear Voice

A clear voice is singing,
and the next signpost has the name of your destination;
the heirloom you'd lost is suddenly in front of you;
the friend you offended sees the joke.

A clear voice is singing,
and the telephone rings in counterpoint;
the girl you're in love with says she loves you;
after so many '*No*'s this letter says '*Yes*'.

A clear voice is singing,
and the fog lifts like a window wiped clean;
you raise a glass of water to your lips;
you wake from a dream and the pain has gone.

A clear voice is singing,
and a fist unclenches; an arm relaxes;
the sun rises, someone slips out of life
and dives into a pool.

A clear voice is singing
on the other side of a soundproofed window:
the notes are behind bars.
A tree falls. One hand claps.

Grating

How did you get here? It's clear you started
from your source on the other side,
but there are several entrances. Which did you use?

The portico faces the desert. Near the horizon,
too bright to stare at, is the source. Imagine
someone using a mirror to reflect the sun into your eyes.
Now picture something both more brilliant
and less easy to see. There is no flickering, no variation.
If it loved you, you would already have been seduced.
If the source were your enemy, you'd be dead.

It is important, for the smooth working
of our internal procedures, that we know
between which pillars you passed.

His clothes say fussy little man, who finds
the platypus abhorrent, who's sick in helicopters.
Were his child to be born on a leap day
the official would probably have a nervous breakdown,
and would never forgive his wife.

You must know the one through which you came.
What do you mean that all entrances contributed
to your arrival? You are not making sense.

The visitor is pleasant, relaxed.
He appears to be doing his best,
but his answers could not have been
designed more effectively irritating.

I am perfectly aware that travel can be disorienting.
I cannot accept that if I knew
which entrance you used, that knowledge
would change the manner of your arrival.

The visitor now says something
that provokes the official further,
causing him to jump from his chair,
make extravagant gestures of denial.
No, no, no he appears to be saying.
This is not possible. It is not true.

It is true, though. The point of view
pulls back to reveal another, identical office,
then another, then more and more.
In each, a different official, and in each,
the same visitor, sitting quietly, imperturbable,
having imparted the same information,
with equally startling effect.

Out of focus people

I came from home and I did not belong.
Home was light years away.
Home was just around the corner.
Home was the fragrance of apples and a wide sky maculate with clouds.
Home was an argument the size of a black stone.
I journeyed here and the journey was tedious.
The journey took a thousand years.
The journey took a slammed door and five minutes.
The journey took more than I could afford.
I arrived and realised I do not belong.
I arrived without money or the necessity for money.
I arrived without power, but I do not need power.
I claim by right of conquest, anyway.
I want to be friends.

Package

Mass-produced automata packed into
nine-abreast endless ranks of the inevitably
delayed flight all we want is sleep
all they want is to say fasten your safety
belt in the unlikely event we will be issuing
headphones fit your own before assisting a
romantic comedy starring and directed by
breakfast followed by your choice of tea or
charity scratchcards followed by an altitude
of duty free miles per hour and followed by
the ground temperature in fucking Cairo.

Washrooms going down like flies and queues
getting longer. Clear air turbulence: the captain
has switched on the seatbelt sign and someone is
an unpleasant shade of green. *We do apologise. Nevertheless.*
I'M SORRY BUT I'M GOING TO THE TOILET.

We do hope you have enjoyed your flight.

Hands

The rumour of my birthday has spread
and they have given me a present of hands.

The girls have cajoled everyone into covering
palm and fingers with paint and pressing them onto this sheet.

Now, they've brought the painting to me
and I haven't enough of the right words to give back.

I have all the hands to touch.
I can fit my own against any of them.

Turning the sheet around and around
I can read the names. All of them.

They've used determination and charm and youth
to collect the whole set.

They have brought it to my room and told me solemnly
about where it's still a bit wet from the last hand they caught.

I say thank you and thank you and it isn't enough.
Even the dog has left his paw print.

No Sign

There's nothing in the flight patterns
of migrating birds, of arrangements of tea leaves
or intestines. Domestic animals are not behaving

out of character. The women's courses
are reliable. No salt has been spilled;
the mirror over the fireplace

is unsplintered. The crackle of the fire itself is not
malicious. Let it burn out, if you will, examine
the ashes. You will find nothing.

The runes fall uncontroversially. Cobwebs are spun
with no cabbalistic signs even the longest-
nosed of your adepts can detect.

Rain falls and sun shines in appropriate measure
for the time of year. Gravid cows give birth to
unmonstrous, single-headed calves.

There is nothing in the newspapers or the crystal ball.
There are no children with unusual birthmarks;
not a suspicion of a comet or a black cat.

The oak remains unshivered by lightning.
Everyone has his horseshoe nailed above his door,
and if he carries charms, carries them secretly.

Up on the hill, Joe dreams his dreams
and his son sees visions but that's just
henbane, and too long without a woman.

The dogs are quiet at night.

The Fabric Torn

Human skin is a major component of dust.
So, the armada of glittering specks that sails,
An invasion of alien life-forms, out of the sky
To settle on the semi-detached, the tent,
Or the shanty, may well be in part the ghost
Of a friend, or an enemy, coming out of the sun.

All your life, I have warned you, beloved but prodigal son,
How shortly your bones and bowels will be once again dust.
So make it your own: don't let your life be ghost-
Written. Be sure that your chosen ship, when it sails,
Has you at its helm. Now, pack up your tent.
Unfurl your beautiful wings; launch into the sky.

The eagle searches the earth from the comforting sky.
The unreasonable hero steals fire from the core of the sun.
These reinforced walls are no more than the skin of a tent.
Their intricate plans are nothing but drawings in dust.
A life's worth is merely the bankable profit on sales.
How does it all look from where you are, ghost?

"How easy it is to make a ghost."
These great machines, elephantine in the sky.
(Marvel at their slow majesty as they sail,
In fascination, beggaring the sun.)
Then nothing, apart from smothering dust
And a child crying, outside a tent.

You have ripped the fabric of your enemy's tent.
You have struck at his soul, sent his screaming ghost
To the moon's condolence. You have raised such blistering dust
As will blind the face of a scarred and bewildered sky,
Discourage the round, white disc of the sun,
Set great cities falling like crumpled sails.

In your wisdom, do you foresee what sails
Into the night? Will you hide in the dark of your tent,
Hoping the scouring eye of the sun
Won't rise tomorrow, or will be a mere ghost
Flickering harmlessly past in the sky,
Missing you, insignificant speck in the dust?

Or could it be that what sails is your ghost?
Do you know its intent? Under what sky
Will you next see the sun? Eating what dust?

Good Luck, Mr Gorsky

Just by reading this, you've invited Satan onto your computer's hard disk
and the authorities now have you down as a potential security risk.

But you're ok, Mr Gorsky. We confirm receipt of your note:
it was some other burglar's finger stuck in the Doberman's throat.

The fire insurance policy claim
for the smoked cigars was filed in a different name.

And Mrs G? Well, you don't get on as well as you might,
but at least she wasn't locked in a trunk on her wedding night.

She never dried her hair in the microwave, nor is it true
she spread contraceptive jelly on toast and then tried to sue.

She knows about dioxins in tampons; you should have seen her face
when she read there's also a cynically inserted asbestos trace.

But she can tell feminine deodorant from glitter hair spray
or peanut butter (which the dog hates, anyway).

Speaking of the dog, we trust that it hasn't as yet
been hit by that frozen urine ejected by a jet,

or hidden under your 4x4, injured, aggrieved,
with the fizzing stick of dynamite it's retrieved.

The stolen cow thrown out of the transport plane
at 30,000 feet, missed. This time. Someone might try again.

The hospital cleaner, needing a socket, didn't disconnect
your life support system. We checked.

You may have smuggled your dead mother over the border,
but your caravan wasn't stolen, at least, not by our order.

Cyanide in the ATM deposit envelope glue
was, honestly, never going to be an issue for you.

You wouldn't risk bad luck by breaking the chain.
When your stolen car is returned, the front seat will contain no champagne.

You were nowhere near Roswell. We do hope you agree.
When the cookie crumbles, don't ask for the recipe.

Paramount Studios is making this into a movie? They might.
One more thing: aren't you glad you didn't turn on the light?

The Arachnids of Lynn (KL5)

The sky is trying hard this evening. One particular
orange-mauve-pink tempts me back to Do-It-All
to see if I can get a matchpot to match. They have stopped

selling tarantulas at Do-It-All. It seems too many people
bought them without knowing The Care and Attention of,
and they all ended up at the RSPCA. There must have been

hundreds arriving by every post, spilling out of
filing cabinets, blocking the drains. You can understand
how the RSPCA might have got shirty, put the screws on.

How difficult can it be to look after tarantulas?
You just feed them whatever it is they eat. The occasional
small child, probably. I've heard they go splat

if you drop them. Perhaps that's it. In Tesco's cafe,
I'm eating a Big Brunch, and feeding chips
to the tarantula under the table. I could have had

chicken curry, but everyone knows the spices
don't agree with tarantulas. Although it rained earlier,
the clouds no longer have the look of rain.

I've misjudged the time I needed to kill.
There's an unattractive hour kicking its legs feebly
in front of me. Like a neglected tarantula.

Did I need to say that? Could I have left it
as an unresolved reference for you to pick up
and enjoy the discovery?

The car park is nearly deserted. A couple
are decanting a baby into their car. The quay's
been done up nicely with statues and plaques

and bits of maritime equipment too big to steal.
Not many places for tarantulas to call home.
Someone should have thought of installing nesting boxes.

The couple have driven away with their baby,
rear fog light on, although it's not foggy. Just in case, I expect.
There'll be one happy tarantula tonight.

Why is that other car parked on a grassy knoll,
lights on, engine running, woman passenger eating
chips, her man watching, hirsute arms

crooked on the steering wheel? Why go to the trouble
when the car park is just a few yards, and free after six.
Here, on the quayside, under soft tones

of a high pressure sodium lamp, tarantulas scuttle
into shadows, or hide motionless
beneath scant, cultivated undergrowth.

It is time to go in.

diesDeparmen ea spia Auriy d and Enirnme na ygiene eparmen ecemer 1994 (1seiin) M ay 1997 (2neiin) Nemer 1999 (3reiin) 1ae Cnens ae Cnens1Inru cin an Caegrizain 2R

ecmmene rceures: A. as ice sa . recauin s r mruary sa C. recauins r sa nera arrs /nerakers . recains recmmene r reaies ee a E. Acciena exsre r y is 7101215Aenix 1

: recainary measres r aning ea ies 16Aen ix 2 : Sames sickers cains r aning an is sa a is Inrcin A a is ar niay incis an i as.Ag ms rgaisms , sm icis ags ay rasi r

) 9 2 2 0 92 3 3 3 : 2 z 3 0 / 2 3 2 2 2 2 j - 2 & 3 2* - z- J 3* z- J * / : : ::

edge

moon spells other than blood
in a rocking-house bind
silicon grates a salt-water
dance on your unshoes

fall in the shimmer-scape race
to the greensticks up
a plasticiser double-wrack
a carving out of love

that slipshod millennia or worse
article down-wing sibilant
strain stench turn glide
unyielding empty crate

fact upon bureaucratic fact
into the ache and the metal
only knowing string-burn
a pebble in the palm of your hand

I have said nothing...

I have said nothing, up to now,
about the ceremony.
No word of the

nervousness attendant upon
the ritual appraisal of
fellow penitents

waiting to learn into which hands
their futures will be
commended.

I have remained silent on matters
concerning the ascent
to the chair;

the levitation; the queries that require
prescribed responses;
the damping down;

identification of the parting; the time
spent watching your reflection
change, as your soul

falls, scatters onto
borrowed robes,
onto the floor.

I have not touched upon that dangerous part,
near the end, when you are caught
between two mirrors.

I have not spoken of the neophyte sweeping
your grey together with the black,
red and gold.

For what purposes and for whose profit this will be,
I dare not say. You can be certain
it will not be for yours.

And emerging into a colder world that
no longer quite recognises you:
I have not mentioned that.

Eclipse

Suppose it didn't go quite as expected:
when darkness came, a sound of tortured gears
shrieked out and human hands clapped human ears
the whole world round. And then these words, inflected
by some chrysostomatic soul, directed
(no doubt) by God to calm His peoples' fears:
Your forefathers were right - but crystal spheres
can slip sometimes and have to be corrected.

Then silence. Then the moon resumed her pace
as smoothly as the pickpocket who's lift-
ed all of it. Nothing to do but sift
dust vainly. Cruel? Well, a different joke's
this: at totality, a grinning face,
and under it skywriting. *That's all folks.*